T0151087

BOOKS BY BARBARA JANE REYES

To Love as Aswang (PAWA, 2015)
Diwata (BOA Editions, Ltd., 2010)
Poeta en San Francisco (Tinfish Press, 2005)
Gravities of Center (Arkipelago Books, 2003)

INVOCATION TO DAUGHTERS

CITY LIGHTS SPOTLIGHT SERIES NO. 16

BARBARA JANE REYES

INVOCATION

TO

DAUGHTERS

CITY LIGHTS

SAN FRANCISCO

CITY LIGHTS SPOTLIGHT
The City Lights Spotlight Series was founded in 2009,
and is edited by Garrett Caples.

Library of Congress Cataloging-in-Publication Data
Names: Reyes, Barbara Jane, author.
Title: Invocation to Daughters / Barbara Jane Reyes.
Description: San Francisco : City Lights, [2017] | Series: City Lights
Spotlight ; 16
Identifiers: LCCN 2017023929 | ISBN 9780872867475 (paperback)
Subjects: | BISAC: POETRY / American / Asian American.
Classification: LCC PS3618.E938 A6 2017 | DDC 811/.6--dc23
LC record available at https://lccn.loc.gov/2017023929

Cover Image: *Do you have a Filipina* [detail] (2010) by Mel Vera Cruz.
Copyright © 2010 by Mel Vera Cruz.

All City Lights Books are distributed to the trade by
Consortium Book Sales and Distribution: www.cbsd.com

For small press poetry titles by this author and others,
visit Small Press Distribution: www.spdbooks.com

City Lights Books are published at the City Lights Bookstore,
261 Columbus Avenue, San Francisco, CA 94133
www.citylights.com

CONTENTS

Give your daughters to us,
and take our daughters for yourselves.

— Genesis 34:9

If I had wings I would fly, let me contemplate . . .

— Warren G

INVOCATION TO DAUGHTERS

FAQ

1. *Are you fluent in your mother tongue? What is your mother tongue?*

I am fluent in the language of la luz, ang lakbay, el cruzamiento. My mother tongue is criollo y kimera; it is also mongrel and bastard. The tongue is not déficit but prisma, and light (in)forms its root and offshoot. It is sometimes called refraction. Ang aking gramatika, un arco iris.

Madre mía migrante, señora, doña. Lenguaje ay wikang casa, wikang esposa, wikang ciudad, wikang trabajo, y wikang mundo. Yes, I am fluent in my mother's tongue.

2. *Don't you worry that other people might not understand you?*

People will come to understand what they want to understand. Those who know una significado es ilusyon (o delusyon), ang intindi ay simaron, they know liminaridad. The ones who demand understanding en una lengua, the ones who demand una kortada ng dila, the ones who request una violencia de la media lengua, intolerante. They really want obediencia. Di ba? They want me to be their mono. Mga suplado. Reklamo-reklamo. Xenófobo. Ako po ay sigurado.

3. *Why are you so angry? Don't you ever smile?*

Why aren't you angry? Why does my outrage inconvenience you? Why is my resting bitch face your concern?   Are you afraid of me?

Who told you that a lady should always smile, and for whose benefit and pleasure would that be? Why did you believe them? Why do you believe them still?

4. *Why can't you just write about beautiful things?*

Voz is beautiful. Home is beautiful. Lenguaje is beautiful. Grit is beautiful. Orasyon is beautiful. Daughter is beautiful. Kuwento is beautiful. Safety is beautiful.

Do you see the woman fighting for air? Do you see the woman guarding her kin? Do you see the woman learning to speak? Do you see the woman resisting being broken?

If you do not see the beauty in these, then I am sorry for you.

5. *Why don't you just say what you mean?*

That's what I do. Siempre and siyempre.

INVOCATION TO DAUGHTERS

Daughters, our world is beyond unkind. We know it is downright brutal. We have no haven; we have known only words for our bodies such as commerce, coercion.

A passive language strips us of our kick and grit and fight in our bloodlines. A vulgar language attributes our survival to others' benevolence, belying our scars' true, cruel sources. A language of consumption frames our humanity as thighs, breasts, and eggs. A language of proprietorship brands and cages us.

We are una herida abierta, isang bukas ng sugat.
We are una lengua quebrada, isang putol na dila.
We are piraso, parsela, objetos para komersyo.

Daughters, the fathers monitor our developing curves, control our bodies, redact consent from our tongues. They deem us deficient, dirty.

Daughters, our kind is now endangered; we are dying young and desperate, and no words were ever ours.

Daughters, let us create a language so that we know ourselves, so that we may sing, and tell, and pray.

THE GOSPEL OF MARY JANE

Isa rin akong babae na may pangarap
I am a lady who has ceased to be
Alam ko kung gaano ang hirap
A lady, your lessened abjectee

Isa rin ako sa inyo nakipagsapalaran
I am a lady, no more than symbol
Pag-asa ng ating bayan
Homeless hope of our hapless people

Marami man pong hindi naniniwala
I am a lady, fighting for my life
Na wala akong kasalanan
Servile, unmeant to survive

Alam nang Panginoong Diyos na
I am a lady, writing for my life
Nagsasabi ako nang katotohanan
This anti-silence is my right

(All ages to come shall call me blessed)

MYTHOS

Fulcrum

The daughter's body is the fulcrum of the father. She is burdened and dirt. She is vulnerable. The daughter's body is the water of the father. She is watched and walled. She is inaudible. The daughter's body is the artifice of the father. She is parcel and article. She is vernacular. The daughter's body is the sediment of the father. She is silt and salt. She is unsentimental. The daughter's body is the prism of the father. She is precious and prig. She is pregnable. The daughter's body is the shears of the father. She is shrill and jilt. She is spectacle. The daughter is the language of the father. She is latent and gauge. She is translatable.

Cancer

The daughter's body is the cancer of the father. She is callused and cowed. She is antithetical. The daughter's body is the platform of the father. She is bland and blanked. She is implantable. The daughter's body is the loophole of the father. She is foolish and foul. She is unlovable. The daughter's body is the incisor of the father. She is biting and bile. She is stifled. The daughter's body is the simulacra of the father. She is simplistic and small. She is lachrymal. The daughter's body is the preservative of the father. She is pert and pristine. She is vestigial. The daughter's body is the arsenal of the father. She is source and sinner. She is archetypal.

Collateral

The daughter is the collateral of the father. She is worth most on the market if pure. The daughter is the merchandise of the father. She is properly trained in housewivery. The daughter is the consequence of the father. She is one too many mouths to feed. The daughter is the failure of the father. She is tits and hips, a uterus to fill. The daughter is the error of the father. She is hidden away from the world. The daughter is servant of the father. She is also her brothers' nursemaid. The daughter is the burden of the father. She is quietly planning her exit.

Domain

The daughter's body is the domain of the father. She stages rebellion, he cannot withstand. The daughter's body is the name of the father. She revokes her oath and casts new spells. The daughter's body is the rule of the father. She buries his empire's rotting carcass. The daughter's body is the will of the father. She stanches its flow and watches it wither. The daughter's body is the regiment of the father. She aims with the kill shot, one by one. The daughter's body is the swagger of the father. She punctures his ego's tender skin. The daughter's body is the jurisdiction of the father. She excises herself from his tyranny.

Appendage

The daughter is the appendage of the father. She severs herself, she grows her new parts. The daughter is the projection of the father. She dims his light to a tiny, cold flame. The daughter is the amplification of the father. She bursts his lungs and savors the quiet. The daughter is the instrument of the father. She sharpens herself against his attacks. The daughter is the explanation of the father. She unbinds herself from his censure. The daughter is the footnote of the father. She delivers herself from his skull. The daughter is the transgression of the father. She slays the man so the girl child may live.

SOME GUIDELINES FOR WOMEN

AFTER TOMAS AND PILAR ANDRES

Below are some don'ts for women to avoid getting into "trouble"*:

1. A woman should not try; she might end up in trouble*.
2. She should not wear attire that reveals shape or skin; it is an invitation to trouble*.
3. She should not be expressive, emotional, or opinionated.
4. She should not act. She should allow others to presume what is best for her.
5. She should not feel silly sitting passively. Men will want to open her.
6. A woman should just let them.
7. A rich woman should not isolate herself from working women. The more she employs the domestic services of, for example, Filipino women, the easier her life will be, and the better she will feel about her own station.
8. She should smile when told she should have children, she should have more children (especially sons), she should be caring for the children of others. She may try to change the subject, but she should smile when doing so.

9. She should not drive herself; she should never literally or figuratively take the wheel.
10. She should not feel disturbed to be taken lightly.
11. She should never look you directly in the eye. It is a gesture of equality, and it is therefore an invitation to trouble*.
12. She should be indexed. She is preferable downward. Otherwise, she is considered rude.

* Examples of "trouble," include but are not limited to the tarnishing of name, spinsterhood, abandonment, verbal, emotional, and/or physical harassment or abuse, aggravated assault, abduction, date rape, acquaintance rape, spousal rape, employer rape, gang rape, false imprisonment, sexual slavery, forced abortion, human trafficking, premature death by cruel, violent, and undignified means, including immolation and dismemberment.

GLORIA PATRI

glory be to the father who oversees   your virtue   your bodily
fluids   your menstrual cycles   your engorged glands   glory be
to the father   the son is always preferred

glory be to the father of a bridled and properly wived you   a
penetrable you   a bleeding breeder   a penned beast dispensed to
the highest beater

glory be to the who's your daddy asshole son-in-law loser
boyfriend pervy uncle lord savior pimp and not-so-moneyed
john   who pull strings and push skin   whose greasy hands grab to
sample the goods   whose public comments regarding the ripeness
of your breasts hips and ass you must accept   whose rights demand
your hymen intact   who master your hyster(i)a   who invade,
occupy, claim jurisdiction over your fallopian tubes and every
precious ovum

there are many yous   younger flowering wombs to be filled   to
bear the boys   this is the word of the lord

there is no you for you   there is no no for you   this is the word of
the lord

as it was in the begging is known and ever shall be his wor(l)d
without and or amend

amen

PRAYERS OF PETITION

1. To the Patron Saint of Husbandry and Harness Makers
With Arlene Biala, Veronica Montes, and Jay Santa Cruz

Please do not shush her when she speaks.
You nitpick every little thing; you make her small.
Please do not tell her she doesn't know anything.
You are not pleased; she does nothing right.
Please do not tell her she should smile.
You are her master; this is tradition.
Please do not tell her her skin is too dark.
You pull her hair; you throw her to the floor.
Please do not tell her she is a fat cow.
You do what you will; no one will stop you.
Please do not leer at her body parts.
You beat down the door when she changes the locks.
Please do not leer at her daughters.
You own her; everything she has is yours.
Please do not grab at her body parts.
You make her suffer; you knock out her teeth.
Please do not grab at her daughters.

You promise to change; next time will be different.

Please do not block her with your body.

Your home and your castle, your family values.

Please do not cut off her hair.

You shoot, you strangle, you beat her up.

Please do not tell her to calm down.

You bludgeon, you burn; you serve no jail time.

Please do not pretend she did not say no.

You are not to blame; she stays, doesn't she.

Please do not stab her, then call her your soul mate.

You don't need to change; the laws favor you.

Please do not tell her it will be OK.

You turn on the charm; you know she'll come back.

Please do not tell her not to tell anyone.

You take away her money; she has nothing without you.

Please do not tell her not to make a scene.

You break her spirit; you tease her with hope.

Please do not tell her she's crazy.

You grip your pistol, your fist, your baseball bat.

Please do not incapacitate her.

You know she will stay, for better or for worse.

Please do not lock her in your closet and starve her.

You post bail easy; it's always this way.

Please do not penetrate her against her will.

You drink, and you fuck her so hard, you rip her.

Please do not impregnate her against her will.

You punch her first trimester belly, this is not your problem.

Please do not set her body on fire.

You dump her body — trash, woods, don't matter.

Please do not blame her for her death by your hands.

You are a disease; we will eradicate you.

2. To the Patron Saint of Encumbered Wives

Hija con la barba, pray for us
Bearded maiden of the cross, we have
Many stake claim upon us
No sanctuary from the fathers' will
Santa Librada, crucificada
Our husbands' whims, and our sons
This burden of patriarchs
Ravaging the sad vessels of namesake.
Hija con la barba, virgo fortis
Bearded maiden, they say you are myth,
Corseted messiah, bogeywoman
They brand us cult of hysterical girls,
Sacrilegious sister, que bárbara
They smash our faces with their fists
We are the encumbered wives
They shove our bodies, they spit on us.
Hija con la barba, cut us loose
Bearded maiden, we are ungraced

Unwive our brutish husbands
We are wretched bitches, we are used.
Santa patrona de la tribulación
We will be a woven phalanx of women,
Wild-haired protector, we stand
With you, interlocked. With you, holding.

SHE IS

Patron Saint

Patron saint of every victim, every plain Jane
Doe, every Juana de la Cruz. Her real name?
Who cares. What matters is she is female,
She is poor. She is patron saint of the humbled,
She is a martyr doing right. She is always poor.
She is Christian. She is poor. She is coerced.
She is the grateful, weeping daughter
Patron saint of rosaried, weeping mothers.
What if she were impure in thought and body,
Sharp-tongued, willful. What if she didn't pray.
What if she were hard, what if ill-meaning,
What if she fought back, what if she declined
To be your victim. So what if you call her
Ingrata. What if she knows herself. What if.

Ingrata

Ingrata, what if she knows herself. What if
She were bleeding from her larynx, crushed
Slumped beside the toilet, dragged and dragged.
So what if you made her lungs ooze and swell,
So what if you punched her, choked her, ended
Her life — what you would not truly call a life,
This ruptured thing, this scalpeled two spirit.
To aspire is to breathe, is to desire,
Is to soar, is to hope, is to rise
As smoke, is to crave, is to fight for air
When the larynx is crushed and voice is lost.
But what if she could speak. Then you would know
She never feared you. This is no metaphor —
Just another body, just another day.

Spreadeagle

Just another body, just another day
For slut shaming, too sexy, too full
In the lips, tempting. Lipsticked whore, so what
If her skirt's too short, if her neckline's low.
So what if you think she's hot. She is hot.
So what if she's spreadeagle, inhaling
Mud. So what if you forced her down, so what
If she said no, and no again, fat lipped,
Bleeding, clawing for life. They will say
She deserved it. They will say she made you
Strip her down, break her bones and thrust,
All of you, boys will be boys will be
Forgiven, led to lust by ripened breasts,
Fleshy pomes, for tongues, sharp teeth, hunger.

Monstrous

Fleshy pomes, for tongues, sharp teeth, hunger —
What if we are monsters, selvedged selves,
So many throwaway pieces to stitch.
So what if we are monstrous, fear making,
Howling, disobedient, salvaje. So what
Of our hunger, for breath, for space to nurse
The hurt, the blame, the unnaming of us,
The harvesting of parts, the cleaving. Yes,
What if we were monsters, cackling, joyous,
Revelers, rebels. So what of your fear,
Of witches, of putas who speak our minds,
Who touch the earth, unbound, backbones bridging,
Whose lyrics break, brave, brassy, and bright.
So what if you call us bitches. Who cares.

Bitches

So what if you call her a bitch, who cares.
What if she speaks her mind without fear,
What if we all could be so brave. So what
If she curses. What if she resists, yes,
Fights back. What if her tiny body roars,
Stands tall, holds her fists, and waits. Just waits.
What if we all could be so solid, still,
Weighing each word, each soundly voiced oath.
She is through with your shit, every insult,
Every threat you level, every dirtbag
Attack can't move her. What if we all could
Stand with her, what if we all could fight back,
Yes, defend our sister against assault,
Each one of us so capable, who knows.

Brown Girl

Each one of us so capable, who knows
About a skin and bones brown girl, captive.
The avenues know where she turns her tricks,
That budding bodies bring the big bucks.
Who cares that she is some sad mother's
Lost daughter, taken, drugged, and dirtied,
Tattooed *bitch* on her breaking breastbone.
Your abandoned animal, so desperate —
See her glassy eyes, there's nothing there,
Just some thing to blow you. She is fast, cheap,
And easy, so who cares that she's hungry.
The avenues know this traffic of girls,
Always plotting escapes, so filled with dreams
Of baring their claws, of biting down hard.

Punyeta

She is baring her claws, biting down hard,
She-beast clamping down on her kill. She is
Monstrous, mended; she is breathing fire,
Purging, and from ash, she is blessing.
She is bruja y puta, she is through
With your shit. Tarantada, punyeta,
Each and every repieced piece of her speaks,
Amen! Each wrinkle, each scale, horn, and thorn,
Each tangle, each scowl, each middle finger
She flips, unfurls. She spits hard, she howls long
Lament. She wails low from the belly,
Hear this hymn, this naming song, this psalm.
She is knowing, holy, protector and
Patron saint of every victim, every plain Jane.

ORASYON

I.

María santisima, maravillosa
She is a fissure, an excess
María, aming ina imakulada
She is an absence manifest

María divina, mahal na diwa
She is a myth, a missing thing
María, isang niña embarazada
She is blistering, she is stilled

2.

Mother most filled and giving
Kayo'y perla del mar oriental
Mother most civil and willing
Kayo'y siguradong umaandar

Mother most wise and graced
Kayo'y pinakamahal ng patria
Mother most fair and praised
Kayo'y imperyalistang obra maestra

3.

Our Lady most annealed
Naghihintay/estoico
Our Lady most bereaved
Nagbibigay/generoso

Our Lady of hone and keen
Nahihiwalay/apartado
Our Lady of stone and bleed
Namamatay/moribundo

4.

Pray for us, grinding hustler
Aming ina, migrante eterna
Pray for us, most shrewd mother
Aming balyenteng trabajadora

Pray for us, worker of the world
Aming guardia ng amor propio
Pray for us, industrious lamb of God
Aming garantía sa paraiso

5.

Maria ng kusina ng mundo
Lady who must know her station
Maria ng kubeta ng mundo
Lady aching, self-effacing

Maria, dalaga, sobra coqueta
Lady whose virtue is bittersweet
Maria, mas blanca, mas bella
Lady of burning, lady of bleach

6.

Mater purissima, Mater castissima
Pray for us, our sharpest razor
Mater inviolata, Mater intemerata
Pray for us, brassy ball breaker

Mater cruci, Mater dolorosa
Pray for us, our lady most hewn
Mater lacrimosa, Mater afflicta
Pray for us, third world drug mule

7.

Our lady of absolute obedience
Isang babae, hija ng imperyo
Our lady of confession and lament
Isang babae, anak ng dominado

Our lady of derelict language
Isang babae, kortada ng lengua
Our lady of scavenge and salvage
Isang babae, esposa en la basura

INVOCATION TO DAUGHTERS 2

We mourn for the things that were taken: knowing and name. A body at peace. Our poisons were drained from our secret places.

We are prickly and complicated. Once, we were luminous. Now, we are bitter, and beastly. Once, we were a sight to behold. Now we are endangered.

We mourn our horns hewn from our skulls, ground into powder. We molt our weathered cells to fertilize the earth beneath our bellies.

We creep and contract our bodies until we are armored and brilliant shells. We are salt and sanguine. We are the dark water's weight.

CONSUME

La poesía es como el pan, de todos — ROQUE DALTON

Their bones were thicker and stronger than ours — ARLENE BIALA

The women gather salt in secret caves, in shallow pools of ocean.
The men blast the shoreline and barricade the caves. They force feed
refined white sugar to the soil. What fruit will grow there,

What Satsuma mandarins for Santo Niño, for my father's sepia
portrait and Our Lady of Grace, what altar's dinuguan and steaming
brown rice,

What typhoon relief sacks of GMO rice rotting for vermin, cockroach
crony syncophants to sate themselves,

What banana throwing douchebag bros, what sports stadium military
industrial complex makes me sing, God bless America,

What mofongo de camarones al ajillo y café con leche, please, what
Yankees game's on the TV at Malecon,

What oxtails and bay leaves have been stewing all day, what flesh melting into peanut sauce and achiote. What marrow bones to save for my father,

What bone broth elixir in mason jars, what Whole Foods 100% raw organic coconut water, what juice cleanse won't let me not think you're an asshole,

What bag of liquid nutrition, pumped intervally through a gastric tube. Don't assume it fulfills the dying need,

What last meal on earth if not Jacques Pépin's home-baked bread, with just a little unsalted butter,

What white bread we have, what spamsilog. We have the key to the can of corned beef, maraming salamat, po, Amerikano!

What nutritional value in Guantanamo rectal force feeding, men penetrating men nonconsensually, for "national security,"

What permanent damage done to one's internal organs, what softened bones and ruptured vessels. Don't assume anyone's lost any sleep over this,

What cost prohibitive lipid lowering pharmaceuticals, what BMI plan. What insulin dependent adult onset diabetes. Ischemia and embolus are the new norm.

We are dying for a sweet sip of water, for bread to dissolve on the tongue.

THE GOSPEL OF JUANA DE LA CRUZ

in the beginning with the word, there was
your breakfast, your bed, your benefits package
a woman sent, whose name was Juana
your myths, your medicine, your maid for hire

all things were made by her; and without her
your leisure and pleasure, your cheap labor pool
was not any thing made that was made
your tech, your toys, your purchasing power

inside her, all life, and the life of man
your love, your lunch, your urban renewal
she overcame darkness, she came to bear
your realm, your retail, your dollars at work

she came to give testimony, she was the word
your trinkets, your tongue, your taste for travel
and from her fullness you have all received
your savior, your supper, and always, your succor

THE GOSPEL OF ERASE

1.

she   is   your

naked

non-negotiable

symbol

2.   you

your   you

your   you   you

you

APOCRYPHAL

[uh-pok-ruh-fuh l] *adjective*, of doubtful authorship or authenticity.
False; spurious.
C14: via Late Latin *apocrypha (scripta)* hidden (writings), from Greek,
from *apokruptein* to hide away.

1. *The Gospel of No*

And he will say I am stupid if I do not say yes. "She often prayed
these incidents would not escalate to physical touching," "When she
was alone" "she was vigilant" Let there be consequence to saying no.

And he will think it an act of coyness. "The harassment included, but
was not limited to, nudity, comments of a sexual nature, unwanted
sexual advances, and unwanted touching," Let him promise no one
would believe me.

And he will grow angry should I continue to refuse. "walked into
the kitchen naked and watched Plaintiff cook" "she found him naked
and masturbating." Let him curse, you dumb bitch, you can't do shit.

And he will be bemused that my will is strong. "propositioned
Plaintiff" "to perform 'handwork'." "asked whether she wanted to

earn extra money doing 'massage'." Let him brandish his wealth as his weapon.

And he shall not stop until I acquiesce. "On one occasion, he purposefully bumped into her and rubbed his groin against her." Let there be surprise at this accusation of wrongdoing.

And he will say in my weakness, I will fold. "On at least one occasion, Defendant" "asked Plaintiff" "whether she was masturbating in the shower." Let be this man's penchant for naked coercion.

And he will continue to believe that I mean yes. "Plaintiff" "said no." "Plaintiff" "said no." "Plaintiff" "said no" "sexually hostile work environment." "She" "said no." Let this court of public opinion decide who is right.

2. *The Gospel of Comments Section*

For some reason, I do not believe her.
> *She better have proof; I need it. She's making a money grab. She's an unskilled worker, and she should quit complaining. She's lucky to have a job at all.*

For some reason, her story is doubtful to me.

> *She's lying; I'm not buying. She was not a captive, she could have left. She's like every other Filipino, finding the easiest way to get rich quick and stay.*

For some reason, it took her so long to leave.

> *She's a heartless illegal; she should be grateful and not take advantage. She's poor; she's cheap. She's a bogus lawsuit and immigration fraud; deport her.*

For some reason, she expected something different.

> *She's poor; she has no education. She's a whack job extortionist, looking for big payday. She's corrupt, just like the rest of her third world country.*

3. *Response*

Just give it time, and everyone will forget all about her.
Just give it time, and there will be a new one just like her.

PSALM FOR MARY JANE VELOSO

Praise the monstrous body, too enormous to describe. When the tongue is taken, how may the mouth even try.

Praise the bitch slapped face, the hemorrhaged eyes. The cluster. The clot. We thin our blood, we run. We run, and we always look back.

Praise the trafficked body, the one that is excised. On smartphones, with hashtags, we lament the phantom part.

Praise the foreign object rushing to the heart. That is you, the help, the heroine. We pump our fists for you, *isang bagsak!*

Praise the ever-present lens, the firing squad shoots every curse and plea. Your breath is a miracle, a lifeline, a headline.

The old you is dead. Praise for her soul. We offer to her our last *Lacrimosa*. Praise the new you, the chrysalis, the secluded saint.

Praise you. May you emerge, graced and gospeled. Unjudged, unfallen, and the color of sky.

PSALM FOR JENNIFER LAUDE

In revolt against your body, a teenage boy who thinks he is man can
end you   with his bare hands, he takes your air in exchange for fists,
knees, standard issue boots to your breasts   places his tongue has
tasted.   He baptizes you   in the toilet. He wraps you in   motel linen.

This death shroud   un names   you.

They say there is no word for you in your native tongue. They call you
in verted boy, per version — this light bringing, soul-mate loving,
two-spirit, soft-focused, and sexy. This (mis) trans lated bakla mis
cast a cheap hooker, whore, a ladyboy, a grave mis carriage.

Draw a picture of your own heart's double chambers, its perfumed
twinning atriums. Catalogue what is not theirs. Praise your life-
hunger, the body a trans gression, rapid vessel coursing beyond
know. Praise you, trans cendent binabae, glamour deeper than the
coroner's Y-incision.

AN APOLOGY

FOR NORIFE HERRERA JONES

We didn't shout   in the streets   for you.
There were   no raised fists,   no cameras.
Where the Pajaro River   opens its mouth,

to guide our elders   back to native waters,
there was   no one   to bless your passage.
We didn't fight   for you. We forgot to cast

our nets for you. We didn't know you   were
falling. We should have   caught you. When
we didn't   see you   we blamed   the TV,

when the TV noise   smothered you, when
the TV   forgot to   say your name,   when
you ran, when you broke   into pieces. We

should have recognized your name   as kin.
We should have   raised our voices for you.
We should have   raised   all hell   for you,

whetted our   teeth and talons,   as blades,
as spears. We should have   thundered, so
your spirit   would know   its way   home.

INVOCATION TO DAUGHTERS 3

We are dying in alarming ways, and at alarming frequency; no one bothers to count. We are isolated incidents; we are a nuisance.

We are festering, but easy to ignore. We wring our insides, and we bite our tongues, just as we have been instructed.

We have stopped eating now, and we are cutting, albeit not deep enough. We cry in dark and quiet spaces; no one witnesses anything of consequence.

We are too messed up to matter; we are alone, so many of us, apart, and shushed. We dissolve into the walls.

PRAYER ON GOOD FRIDAY

AFTER XYZA CRUZ BACANI

Mercy Plea

In rising we will restore your life —
in judicial review, in hard luck,
in domestic work, in detention cell,
in penitence, and in procession,
in sign and craft, in the street,
in death row traffic, in gift and token,
in prison wage, in innocence, in hope,
in dropping out, in broken marriage,
in single motherhood, in attempted rape,
in housekeeping, in social emergency,
in mercy plea, in pending execution,   .
in legal appeal, in global outcry,
in rejected application, in abandonment,
in dying we will destroy your death.

Sacrifice

In dying we will destroy your death,
We cannot do, and we do not know,
We cannot promise, we are told,
In penning letters of clemency.
We hold the banner of the innocent,
We exhaust all words, we gather
In the streets, we are all calling.
We trust, and we are broken, hoping
We will be found. We find conviction
In flight, in psalms of justice,
We wait, and we wait. We learn
We cannot trust, not even our own kin —
In our hunger, we are sacrificed.
We die for your sins. We rise again.

Object

We die for your sins. We rise again.
We are objects of your choosing,
We proceed in splendor, glamour.
We are produced by you, fashioned by you,
We act, but only with your permission.
We spread your goodwill, we relish prestige,
We thank you, we thank you, and our God —
We shine with opportunity, we stand tall,
We poise our bodies for your liking,
We smile because it pleases you.
We are budding, fragrant, we are fragile.
We suck in our bellies, and our cheekbones,
We are breathless, hungry, and innocent,
We always say yes, as we must say yes.

God-Fearing

We always say yes, as we must say yes —
We place ourselves in your catalogues
We are good girls, we are pure in the flesh
We pray to find companions like you
We are God-fearing, blessed are the meek
We practice your tongues, we hold our own
We speak only when spoken to (softly)
We do as we're asked, we do as we're told
We promise to keep pristine your domain
We uphold the sanctity of the sacrament
We work hard, we save what we earn
We will always place our family first
We sacrifice, we suffer in Jesus's name
We lay down our bodies, as we must.

Deliver

We lay down our bodies, as we must
We eat and sleep, only when we're allowed
We suffocate, we do not know mercy
We avoid eye contact, we bow our heads
We pray to the Lord, we shall not want
We are unseen, so many of us, hoping —
We examine our scars, all we've absorbed
We are burned, we corroborate wounds
We dress our wounds, we seek legal aid
We deliver our testimony, as we must
We help, we nurse, we shelter each other
We seek comfort, only in ourselves
We are poor, and simple in your eyes
We commit everything to memory

Beatitude

We commit everything to memory
Every lie and categorical denial
Every nonconsensual push and thrust
Every parcel of human traffic
Every plea deal and violation
Every curse, every inventoried bruise
Every one of us entrapped, itemized
Every damned day, we fight and we pray —
Blessed are we, poor and persecuted
Blessed are we, exiled, exhausted
You who profit from our suffering
You who fatten yourselves on our hunger —
Eye for eye, and fracture for fracture
It is written, by our steadying hands.

Howl/Witness/Testify

It is written, by my steadying hand
This sorrowful song, this whispering salve
This narrative of knuckled punches
This raised fist, it is my own. I stand
And I speak, though my bravery wavers
And I stand tall, though you tower above me
And I speak, I grit my teeth, and I breathe
And I close my fists, and I hear my voice
This soothsaying, this hollering me
This lyric-making me, now a dazzling we —
We howl, we witness, we testify
We stand firm, and you cannot break us
We are raw nerves, and we are fire. We rise
And in writing, we restore our lives.

INVOCATION TO DAUGHTERS 4

We are fed up being groped, being entered, being punished, being trashed. We are nobody's fucking things.

We own ourselves. We are ours. We are right to fear anyone believing otherwise.

We revoke our consent, which they have obtained through fraudulent means. This is killing us.

Daughters, the word, "no," has been pried from our jaws. We will wrest it back, and guard it, and wield it as our sharpest tool.

DOVE

1. Diwa

before sound and dream   before speech   before our freedom was
breached   before supply and demand   before this parceled, ancestral
land   before strife and fire, no light, no blight   before empire, no
white flight   before warfare rended us apart   before I split the
lovers' bamboo hearth   before enforcing my borders, torture orders,
hoarding and whoring culture   before I was your capital, collateral,
damaged soul, I was liminal

2. *Amihan*

she flew between sea and sky, full wingspan wild   she lifted herself,
the blue above and beneath her roiling   she dove   she dove, and the
light in her lungs dimmed   she thought her heart would burst   she
saw no resting place   she weaved her body with wind   she called
to sea, pushing through clouds   she called to sky, throat forced
utterance, utterance grown to word   and at her command, the rocks
flew from the hands of the sea   she saw rock and water eddy and
settle   she saw the islands they came to form   this is where my
father was born

WE ARE

FOR MY FATHER, TONY REYES (1942-2015)

1. *Ruckus*

We are worms and dirt, perfumed, verdant
We are born of augur, loss, and constant song

We spill liquid lyric, with river kin spitting
We are born of wet and nest, of precious egg

We swell and heat, from seashells and seeds
We are born of clack and crackle, itchy, kicking

We are salt and rock, hawk, bronze, and heart
We are born of the muck, of ruckus and fuss

2. *Elegy*

We are a trickster's daughters, not a man of letters, a father of no sons. I am telling you this, because you want access to something true and personal about me.

We quarreled epic. Know this. When you ask me if he was a good father, I will tell you, it is true he wanted sons. And so we were his boys, hard-drinking, tough, and foul-mouthed like boys.

We are daughters of a man not godly or erudite, just this man whose hands built things, carved bodies into wood, formed them from clay, watercolored their light. He was never a man of words.

We are daughters of a man who forgot things. He forgot to comb his hair. Sometimes, he forgot language. He did not forget how to breathe, but the labor of it became too difficult.

When nothing else was to be done, we sat his last days by his bedside, cooing and whispering, stroking his hair. That was the first time any soul had ever said of us — *maganda pala pag purong babae.*

THE DAY

two fingers on a pulse like the true point

——ANGELA NARCISO TORRES

gloss of feathers dimmed in the orange quiescence of the sun

——LEHUA TAITANO

a damaged beauty, a music I can't manage, no words

——URAYOÁN NOEL

645 am. The very last meal I had with my father was arroz negro y petrale sole paella, fideua caldosa, pork bellies, okra, and a bourbon elderflower cocktail, in Uptown Oakland at Duende. Four days later, his brain got lost in language. *No words*. His body forgot how to walk and how to swallow. His lungs decided to stop taking air. He never came home. He is on my mind when I go to sleep. He is on my mind when I wake up.

836 am. At the AC Transit 26 bus stop, I am late to my day job. Morning commute reminds me of my father, coconut oil slicked hair behind his ears, duck tail in the back. He ironed the creases in his slacks. He left the house with Ralph Lauren Polo aftershave on his collar. He clipped his Bechtel badge to his pocket protector. Protractor, mechanical pencils, drafting tools arranged within reach,

thermos of coffee in his DYMO labeled briefcase, ten-speed bike to Union City BART station. That was before coconut oil became trendy. That was before the layoffs and unemployment checks. After this, combing his hair became a chore.

902 am. Lehua told me that daughters stolen from their homelands do not lose their power. Their tongues, their palates adapt. New roots and unbloomed buds — bullets — become new spells, new medicine. You do not get lost on an island. You take pieces of it — shell, sand, seed — with you when you must take flight. Jelly jars, perfume vials, Tupperware, Ziploc bags, use what you've got.

1021 am. This is when I learned that if you present at the pharmacy early to purchase your DEA-regulated allotment of pseudophedrine, the pharmacy staff will eye you, speak to you like you are a meth head and a fucking criminal. #FML

1050am. "Izabel Laxamana, a 13-year-old girl in Tacoma, Washington died by suicide after jumping off a highway overpass on Friday, May 29. Days before, Laxamana's father … had reportedly punished her for an unspecified transgression by cutting off her hair and uploading a video to YouTube."

1127 am. I belong in this fluorescent-lit cubicle. The privilege of the fluorescent-lit cubicle, where I thumb through thousand-page, spiral-bound indexes. According to the International Classification of Diseases (ICD-10-CM), F43.20, Adjustment Disorder, Unspecified, includes culture shock, grief reaction, and nostalgia. To be a Pinay daughter is classifiable, diagnosable, reimbursable with the proper documentation. It is a disorder. It requires professional intervention. It may require a prescription. To be a Pinay daughter may be covered by your managed care plan. To be a Pinay daughter should be covered by Obamacare. Please consult your manual.

1153 am. Filipino writers on social media asking me why I must write about Filipino things. Don't I fear being seen only as a Filipino writer. Won't I just write about normal things, universal human truths, love and whatnot. Won't I read the important books they say they intend to write. For sake of bayanihan, won't I hook up a fellow Filipino, introduce them to my non-Filipino publishers.

1214 pm. There are ladybugs on my father's grave.

220 pm. You're all girls? You don't have any brothers? Your poor father. How awful that must have been for him. Your mother never gave him any sons.

222 pm. My sisters and I all kept our father's name.

303 pm. I must tell you that first time I heard Prince's "Controversy," was on KDIA 1310 am in 1981. I was 10, dancing and tingling. I'd never heard anything like this, falsetto, synth, electric guitar, and liminality. Because of KDIA, I know that the following year, The Gap Band dropped *Gap Band IV*. My older sister owned it on vinyl, 33-⅓, gatefold LP. It is a perfect album. Let no one tell you different.

432 pm. I am tired of talking about talking about race. These are the facts: I was born on the same island where my mother was born, where my father was born. Where my mother's mother, and my mother's father, where my father's mother, and my father's father were born. Go back many more generations, and you will find our birthplaces are that very same island. *The true point* should not be why I write this, but how, in whose tongues.

435 pm. You do not get lost on an island.

502 pm. *Two fingers on a pulse.* He was still, breathing when I left his room. He was, and one by one they were wheeling away machines. The blipping monitor told me what my hands felt still. He was warm. He was 73. He was a tough motherfucker, stubborn enough to live

to 100, so that he could grumble and elbow us, so that he could give us mad side eye. Instead, just hum and blip. Hum and blip. *A music I can't manage*. Exhale. *No words*.

524 pm. Sometimes you are damaged. You think poetry will repair you. You think poetry should repair you. You shake your fist at it when it doesn't. You walk hand-in-hand with your damage, into the world. You do not speak. You are surprised when people register you are there.

551 pm. Sometimes I can snap out of invisibility. On 8th and Broadway, Marshawn Lynch and I make eye contact. I refrain from telling him that it's my birthday, and may I please take a selfie with him. Why can't this interaction have happened with Draymond Green instead. #oaktown #DubNation

621 pm. There is no printed news story I can find about Norife Herrera Jones, that does not emphasize her dismemberment, and the esteemed alma mater of her estranged 74-year old white husband, her murderer.

753 pm. You don't have kids? Why don't you have kids? You should have kids. How terrible it must be for your husband. You should

give your husband kids. You are a bad wife. How terrible it must be for your parents. You should give your parents grandkids. You are a bad daughter.

802 pm. Think Tatsuya Nakadai in *Harakiri*, unleashing his no fucks left to give, one man wrecking machine on an entire estate of samurai turned peacetime paper pushers. Dying of boredom and leisure time. The rōnin Nakadai thrusting his katana through hollow armour, keeping it real.

903 pm. *On a pulse* that stopped. The breathing stopped. He was warm, but the breathing stopped. Now he *flies to greet my ancestors, gloss of feathers dimmed in the orange quiescence of the sun there is no need now* for sublingual drops of morphine, for the sleep that let him slip away from us.

905 pm. *I can't manage, no words.*

911 pm. Sometimes you are broken. Poetry won't fix you. Poetry can't fix you. It doesn't have lungs to give you its air. It doesn't have hands to stitch your parts back together. To make you tea. To drive you home.

949 pm. Death row prisoner and human trafficking victim Mary Jane Veloso celebrates women's rights with a prison fashion show. Veloso has just modeled a sheer, embroidered sheath dress at Wirogunan Prison. On death row. Curlicues and up-do, perfect eyebrows and pearl manicure. Always a breath away from the firing squad.

1026 pm. My #WCW Pia Alonzo Wurtzbach's Instagram tells me that she has just learned the proper mechanics of the fast ball. Noah Syndergaard taught her this, for Filipino Heritage Night at Citi Field. In my perfect world, Pia would throw out the first pitch at AT+T Park. Tim Lincecum would still be our ace. He would be the one to teach her how to throw, even though Timmy's "The Freak." Arnel Pineda would sing, "Lights," in the middle of the eighth. All the starstruck Filipinos in the house would radiate so much light, we'd be the fucking Maharlika Nebula Supernova of San Francisco.

1155 pm. I remember holding the dove's warmth in my palms. I was still, it was still, it was waiting for me to unlace my fingers. There, the horizon above a young oak tree, mustard flowers, poppies, and autumn snails, the dove's gentle bones pushed off my palms, into *the orange quiescence of the sun*. This is how I said good-bye to my father — shouting his name at the sky.

1157 pm. I sometimes remember to floss. I always wear socks to bed, even in the summertime. I sometimes build a pillow fort. I always think about that day. That with my mother's permission, they wheeled my father out of the hospital covered in a velvet shroud. That I could not sleep for a long time. That I would not close my eyes. That every night noise might have been him visiting me.

INVOCATION TO DAUGHTERS 5

Glory be to the wild-haired daughter; she is
More golden, more splendid than whiskey.

Glory be to that foul-mouthed, bitchy thing
Who was once a shell that we called a lady.

Let it be known she laughs like a man,
Roaring naked from the belly. Such a sight!

Her entire clan of shrews, hags, and witches
Does this — we howl and we snort unruly,

We push rivers of spirits down our gullets.
Doubled over, we curse and wail in glee —

> *Susmaryosep naman! Talaga,*
> *Itong mga babaeng walang hiya!*

WISDOM'S REBUKE

Out in the open wisdom calls aloud, she raises her voice in the public square; on top of the wall she cries out, at the city gate she makes her speech— PROVERBS 1: 20-21

I am not the polite little colored girl you are looking for. You did not fashion me in your image. It is not my ambition that you glance my way, to acknowledge my foreign face, to learn my barbaric tongue, to cherish my diminutive body. You are not my gravity.

I am not your ethnic spectacle. I am not your cultural poverty. You don't get to frame me.

I do not ask for your permission to speak. I do not ask you to hear me. I write whether or not you invite my words. I will not be housebroken, ador(n)ed for my tameness. I am not afraid of you.

You don't get to catalogue me. You don't get to warehouse me. You don't get to rescue me. You don't get to touch me. You don't get to explain me. You are not the standard by which I judge my own worth. You don't get to draw my boundaries.

Fuck your tender fences and applause.

I do not ask for your acceptance. I am not your child. I am not your pet. I am not your object lesson. I don't need your absolution.

TAGALOG NOTES

"Isa rin akong babae na may pangarap ... Alam ko kung gaano ang hirap ... Isa rin ako sa inyo nakipagsapalaran ... Pag-asa ng ating bayan ... Marami man pong hindi naniniwala ... Na wala akong kasalanan ... Alam nang Panginoong Diyos na ... Nagsasabi ako nang katotohanan," are excerpts from Mary Jane Veloso's handwritten letters which she wrote prior to her scheduled (and later stayed) execution. My translation is as follows: "I am also a woman with dreams / I know how difficult it is // I am one of you who risked / The hope of our nation // There are many who do not believe / That I am without fault // The Lord God knows / I am speaking the truth."

"Maganda pala, pag purong babae," It is beautiful after all, to have all girls (daughters).

"Susmaryosep naman! Talaga, / Itong mga babaeng walang hiya!" Jesus, Mary, and Joseph! Really, these women with no shame!

ACKNOWLEDGMENTS

Thank you to the folks who supported and inspired me through the process of beginning and ending this work. Kuwentuhan, the Poetry Center at San Francisco State University, and the Creative Work Fund: Arlene Biala, Javier O. Huerta, Urayoán Noel, Aimee Suzara, Lehua Taitano, Angela Narciso Torres, Steve Dickison, and Elise Ficarra. PAWA, #decolonizepublishing #allpinayeverything #aswangpoetics: Jason Bayani, Tara Betts, Rose Theresa Booker, Amalia Bueno, Rachelle Cruz, Kenji Liu, Karen Llagas, Edwin Lozada, Lisa Suguitan Melnick, Veronica Montes, Conrad Panganiban, Craig Santos Perez, Tony Robles, Janice Sapigao, Melissa Sipin, Eileen Tabios, Von Torres, Jean Vengua, Sunny Vergara, Yael Villafranca, Bryan Thao Worra. And always, my mother, my sisters. And always, Oscar Bermeo.

Thank you to the editors of the following publications in which some of these poems have previously appeared, some in earlier versions: *Delirious Hem*, *Hinchas de Poesia*, *The Margins*, *Prairie Schooner*, *Raven Chronicles*, *South Dakota Review*, *Vector Press*, and in the anthologies *IMANIMAN: Poets Writing in the Anzaldúan Borderlands*

(Aunt Lute Books, 2016), and *Golden State 2017: The Best New Writing from California* (Outpost19, 2017).

"The Gospel of Erase," includes text from "Oriental Girls: The Ultimate Accessory," *GQ Magazine*, October 1990.

"Apocryphal," includes text from *Yang v. Poetzscher and Rao* (2015).

Born in Manila, Philippines and raised in the San Francisco Bay Area, Barbara Jane Reyes is the author of four previous poetry collections, including *Gravities of Center* (Arkipelago Books, 2003), *Poeta en San Francisco* (Tinfish Press, 2005), which received the James Laughlin Award, *Diwata* (BOA Editions, Ltd., 2010), which received the Global Filipino Literary Award for Poetry, and *To Love as Aswang* (PAWA, 2015). She received her B.A. at U.C. Berkeley and her M.F.A. at San Francisco State University. She teaches at University of San Francisco's Yuchengco Philippine Studies Program and currently serves on the Board of Directors for Philippine American Writers and Artists (PAWA). She lives with her husband, poet Oscar Bermeo, in Oakland.

The state of the world calls out for poetry
to save it. LAWRENCE FERLINGHETTI

CITY LIGHTS SPOTLIGHT SHINES A LIGHT ON THE WEALTH
OF INNOVATIVE AMERICAN POETRY BEING WRITTEN TODAY.
WE PUBLISH ACCOMPLISHED FIGURES KNOWN IN THE
POETRY COMMUNITY AS WELL AS YOUNG EMERGING POETS,
USING THE CULTURAL VISIBILITY OF CITY LIGHTS TO BRING
THEIR WORK TO A WIDER AUDIENCE. IN DOING SO, WE ALSO
HOPE TO DRAW ATTENTION TO THOSE SMALL PRESSES
PUBLISHING SUCH AUTHORS. WITH CITY LIGHTS SPOTLIGHT,
WE WILL MAINTAIN OUR STANDARD OF INNOVATION AND
INCLUSIVENESS BY PUBLISHING HIGHLY ORIGINAL POETRY
FROM ACROSS THE CULTURAL SPECTRUM, REFLECTING
OUR LONGSTANDING COMMITMENT TO THIS MOST
ANCIENT AND STUBBORNLY ENDURING FORM OF ART.

CITY LIGHTS SPOTLIGHT